I TALKED WITH SPIRITS

# I Talked with Spirits

VICTOR H. ERNEST

Tyndale House Publishers
Wheaton, Illinois

Coverdale House Publishers Ltd.
London, England

Distributed in Canada by
Home Evangel Books Ltd.
Toronto, Ontario

*Fifth printing, May 1972*

*Library of Congress Catalog Card No. 78-112665*
*SBN No. 8423-1550-0*

*Copyright © 1970 by Tyndale House Publishers*
*Wheaton, Illinois 60187*

*Printed in the United States of America*

*Dedication*

*This book is affectionately dedicated
to my loving and faithful wife for the
stand she has taken with me
in recognizing the power of the Holy Spirit.
Without her unselfish devotion
this book might never have been completed.*

# contents

## foreword

*The Bible tells us plainly there will be a great increase in demon activity as we approach the end of human history. The Apostle makes specific reference to this in 1 Timothy 4:1. The Book of Revelation, chapters 16 and 18, predicts almost universal demonic domination in the final days of God's judgments on the earth. This surge of demonism will be amazingly deceptive, luring the masses and even converting nominal Christians. Veneration for the evil spirits will lead to depraved conduct, and the pinnacle of demonic achievement will be their control of world leaders. As incredible as it may seem, this revelation from the Word of God assures us that dependence on these unseen spiritual forces will increase even as scientific knowledge is increasing.*

*The author of this book is a faithful minister of the gospel and my dear brother in the Christian faith. He writes from his own experiences and intensive study in order that others might not become ensnared in the cult of spiritualism.*

*The book is valuable both as an exposé of insidious spiritualism and a scriptural study of some of the signs of the end times.*

*I trust that it will be widely read and prayerfully observed.*

John B. Houser, Pastor
First Baptist Church
Corvallis, Oregon

## preface

*My primary object in writing this book is to demonstrate the reality and power of evil spirits. I want to share how I became involved in communication with evil spirits, how these spirits—both appealing and loathsome—enslaved me, and how Jesus Christ set me free. This is primarily a personal testimony, not a comprehensive treatise on spirit phenomena. I am describing what I know by firsthand experience and the guidance of the Word of God.*

*Spiritualism is very attractive because it promises knowledge of the future and communication with dead loved ones. Many people will be influenced by demonic spirits in this way without realizing it. The late Episcopalian bishop, James Pike, and the famous seeress, Jeane Dixon, are two such people. The only sure guide into the shadowy spirit world is the Bible, and we neglect it at the peril of our souls. We do well to heed this statement by the noted spiritualist, Thomson Jay Hudson, Ph.D., LL.D., in his book* The Law of Psychic Phenomena: *"The man who denies the phenomena of spiritism today is not entitled to be called a skeptic, he is simply ignorant."*

Victor Ernest
St. Paul, Minnesota

*In Appreciation*
*to*
*the gracious pastors and friends*
*across the country*
*who have encouraged this difficult*
*and sometimes hazardous ministry.*

*"Greater is he that is in you,*
*than he that is in the world."*
*1 John 4:4*

*Talking
with
the
dead*

**1** I could hardly wait for the next seance to take place so I could talk to my departed sister . . . six more days seemed like an eternity.

I had no doubt that Iris would be present, though we had failed on the first attempt. I had talked with the spirit world many times in my twenty-one years, just as I talk with anyone else. I had listened to the spirits give lectures, sermons, exhortations, and counsel to the group assembled at our home seances. But I had never tried to talk to a dead person.

My family, especially my mother's relatives, had been involved with spiritualism for several generations. They came to the United States from Holland before the Spanish American War. My father was a very religious man. He often remarked that he would become a spiritualist if any of his five children were to die.

On June 16, 1933, my seven-year-old sister died, and soon afterward a family from nearby Bemidji, Minnesota, told us they had contacted the spirit of my dead sister and that she was eager to talk to us. The whole family was excited, and we agreed to be in Bemidji at the appointed time for the seance.

There were perhaps ten people gathered in the home for the seance. We sat quietly, meditatively, and expectantly. The medium sat at one end of our semicircle of chairs and led us in singing hymns and in prayer.

It didn't seem strange to us to open the seance by saying

the Lord's Prayer. We even ended: ". . . in the name of the Father, Son, and Holy Spirit." A prayer for a seance went like this:

"Eternal God and Father of Lights, we gather as thy expectant children. We are eager to communicate with the spirit world and the spirits of our departed friends and loved ones. We pray that you would look favorably upon us. Bless us this night with communications from our friends in the spirit world. In the name of the great Father of Lights. Amen."

Then we sang familiar church hymns such as: "Face to Face," "In the Garden," "Beautiful Isle of Somewhere," and "Nearer My God to Thee."

While we were singing, the medium slumped into unconsciousness, and before long a strange voice spoke through the medium's lips; it was the control spirit.

"Good evening, my children. There are many of the departed here, and all are eager to speak with you. The spirit world welcomes you to another opportunity to contact your departed loved ones."

We listened eagerly to the spirit as the medium sat limply, eyes closed, in his chair. The spirit said that a family was present whose departed loved one wanted very much to speak with them, but since she had been in the spirit world so short a time she was still adjusting to her new spiritual dimension and would have to communicate the following week. That was a terrible disappointment, and the whole family could hardly wait until the next seance when we could contact our beloved sister.

At the second meeting we encountered another phase of spiritualism, the trumpet seance (sometimes called a seance of vocal revelation). A metal trumpet, made of aluminum or sheet metal, stood upright in a damp saucer on a table in the middle of the room. When the medium entered his trance, the trumpet rose slowly from the table and dipped into a horizontal position. Eerily, it began spinning with a soft whir and moved around the room, stopping at intervals in midair.

I sat rigid in amazement. I saw the floating trumpet, but I could not believe it. The residents of the home seemed to accept the experience as a very common thing.

The trumpet went first to my mother and then to other members of our family. And we heard a voice, supposedly my departed sister's, but at first we could not distinguish the words.

Then the trumpet came to me. My first reaction was to grab it, and I snatched at the mouthpiece, but it darted away with amazing swiftness. I tried again, but it moved faster than I did. The trumpet finally settled directly in front of me, just out of my reach.

Then the control spirit launched into a lecture about my unbelief, speaking through the unconscious medium. He said I must conduct myself in dignity and orderliness if I were to benefit from the meeting. As my emotions subsided, the trumpet hovered closer and closer to me until it was near my ear, its tip stroking my hair in the way my sister used to comb it.

A voice flowed from the trumpet saying, "I love you; I love you." It was supposed to be my sister's voice, but it did not sound like her to me. Everyone else accepted it as Iris's voice, but I was disappointed; it was not Iris. That was the first of many occasions when she supposedly spoke to the family, but I was never convinced.

At later seances an older sister and I were told we could become gifted spirit mediums. By following the instructions of the spirit voice in the seance of passivity we would in time be able to contact the spirits in our own home.

This sister and I began to practice the seance of passivity for five, six, then seven minutes each evening, adding one minute each time. During these periods we tried to blot out every conscious thought from our minds. Eventually we could sit for fifteen- and twenty-minute periods without being distracted by a single conscious thought.

In one of the longer periods, the phenomenon finally took place that we had been waiting for. I witnessed the spirit taking control of my sister as she lost consciousness and a voice completely foreign to her soft contralto boomed out:

"My child, be not afraid. You have done well. Greater things than these you will do if you only believe. Continue in this way, and the marvels of the spirit world will be revealed to you."

With that, the spirit departed and my sister regained consciousness. She asked what had happened, and I told her the words of the spirit. She was thrilled! She had arrived at a coveted place of spiritual development, and from that time on we held seances in our home for other people, with my young sister as the gifted medium.

Some people say this is all a hoax, that spirits do not talk with human beings and that floating objects are mere trickery. I would agree that a great many of the eerie demonstrations we hear about are clever illusions, but I believe on the basis of personal experience and the plain words of Scripture that spirits of the invisible world do communicate with humanity and do wield supernatural power in our visible world. And the ominous truth is that these spirits are not from God, but are fallen angels controlled by Satan. Their unholy mission is to lead human beings—by refined or gross means—away from dependence on God, their Creator, and they are active in spiritualist churches, seances, psychic phenomena, witchcraft, and idol-worship. Individuals and nations who reject God, no matter how educated and prosperous they are, fall prey to the other god, Satan.

*The*
*mysterious*
*seances*

**2** I want to share some of the astounding things that took place in the living room of our Minnesota home. Our family gathered there frequently before going to bed to find out what the spirit world might reveal to us. Here I experienced the six seances of spiritualism: passivity, vocal reality, trumpet revelation, lights, transfiguration, and levitation.

Seances are noted for quietness. As the participants enter and meditate, they block out their tensions, worries, anxieties, and problems. Through mental discipline they try to be as passive as possible, with eagerness and expectation for what the spirit has for them.

Lights are turned down at every seance. Shades are drawn in the daytime and at night. At some places rheostats dramatically control the lighting. Once when I asked a spirit why the lights were turned down, the reply was, "My son, why do you close your eyes when you pray?"

"For better concentration," I said.

"Just so it is," said the spirit, "that you turn down the lights. It is for better concentration."

Seances always start on time. The exact hour is eagerly anticipated. To arrive late would grieve the spirits. Seances have top priority in the plans of those who attend regularly. Young people give the seance priority in their schedules over athletic events and other school activities.

Sometimes the spirit messages came to us in other languages. I remember Spanish, German, French, and the language of the Chippewa Indians being spoken. When we did not recognize the language the control spirit would tell us what it was and would interpret the central message. It often went something like this:

"Jesus is coming soon. He is even now at the threshold of the parapet of the heavenlies awaiting the word of the great spirit of lights. Wherefore, comfort ye one another with these words, and be ye ready; for ye know not what hour he will come."

When I asked the spirit how we could be ready, the answer was always, "Live a good life, my child. Follow in the steps of the master, the greatest medium of all." This was a vague reference to Jesus, without instructing us in what those steps were.

When a medium went into a trance for any length of time, his or her body became very tired, causing the medium to spend a day or two in bed after the seance. Because of this, we could not have a seance as often as we wanted in our home and we went to seances in the homes of other mediums.

I have already described the seance of passivity, the process of blotting out all conscious thought so a spirit can take control of a medium and speak through him, and the demonstration of spirit power at a trumpet seance.

A most striking phenomenon was a seance of vocal reality I witnessed in connection with my deceased great-grandfather and grandfather. Both had been in the Spanish American War; one was a fifer, and the other a drummer. During the seance we heard feet marching in perfect cadence, the music of a fife, and the beat of drums. Each time, the music was a popular tune of the times, "The Girl I Left Behind Me."

I do not know how all these sound vibrations could be

distinctly produced through the vocal apparatus of the medium, but I'm sure they could have been recorded if such were allowed. The spirit constantly reminded us that public manifestations were for a later time, and so we must keep these revelations to ourselves.

I remember when a large reward was being offered to anyone who would contact the spirit of Houdini, the great magician, after his death in 1926. I suggested that it would be simple to contact his spirit and make it known to the public. And with the reward, we could then begin building the First Church of Christ Spiritualist in our town. But we were told once again that, although this was possible, "the time was not yet." I asked the spirit if the time for this would come, and the answer was yes.

The seance of lights was always preceded by a half hour or so of passive meditation during which each person prepared himself by discipline of mind and emotions for the coming of the spirit. In this seance, the darkened room would fill with drifting lights until it became a mass of colors, each light indicating the spirit of someone who had passed on.

Each color had significance. Little blue lights meant that the spirit of a departed baby was present. There were large orange lights and many yellow and green lights. Green represented spirits that were growing or progressing to a higher plane of spiritual development. A white light indicated a spirit that had progressed to the level of the master himself. Spiritual advancement at this level was signified by the size of the white light.

A red light was considered an "evil" spirit. It was greeted in the circle with a gasp of disappointment and sometimes fear. If a red light appeared, all the other lights would disappear, usually ending the seance.

In the seance of transfiguration, the transfigured form of a loved one who has died appears. A pastor friend of mine went to a seance where his deceased mother seemed to appear, clothed with light. She drifted across the room to her son, stopped, and gave him a gentle smile. The medium said she was trying to tell him she was proud he was a minister. My friend impetuously shouted "Mother!" and leaped up to embrace her, only to have her disappear.

Little is known about the seance of levitation. It was practiced only on a limited scale in the seances I attended. Levitation is sometimes called "soul travel," the phenomenon of spirit development whereby a medium or an advanced convert to spiritualism can leave his body by complete yieldedness to a control spirit. He is not completely disunited from his body, but is able to take conscious flight from it to distant places. I experienced this only once: I was taken into the spirit dimension and witnessed indescribable beauties. It's something I don't talk about.

Two people in our spiritualist group entered the state of levitation from time to time. During these periods they could read the headlines of the *New York Times* as it came off the press before it hit the city streets.

Another phenomenon is called an apport. An object is said to be dissolved into invisible form at one point, then carried by the energy of the medium's control spirit to its destination, and materialized there in its original state.

I know of a family in Oregon that abandoned spiritualism and gave up a trumpet that had been used in seances. Later a smaller trumpet turned up at their home. A medium in Nebraska wrote that her control spirit had told her to send another trumpet. According to her, the trumpet was transported by spirit power on beams of light energy.

The January 25, 1945, issue of *The Psychic Observer*, spiritualism's pictorial journal, printed a striking account of an apport in which the medium's control spirit put a much-wanted book on a person's desk from 3,000 miles away. The writer gave a convincing story of the event, though he didn't claim to know how it had happened.

Madame Helena Blavatsky, co-founder of Theosophy, declared an American medium brought to her in a seance the buckle of a medal buried with her father's body in Russia.

Matter is composed of energy, and energy is never destroyed. I have seen Dr. Irwin Moon's laboratory demonstrations at the Moody Institute of Science in which he increases the voltage of an electric current to atom-smashing velocity. Certain elements, when they are bombarded with this electrical force, can be transformed into other elements. Perhaps, similarly, the energy in man can be attuned to a vital spiritual force to make matter invisible. I do not know the explanation of apport, but it should not be ridiculed or ignored.

Spirit writing is accomplished by a medium who possesses the gift of writing while under the power of a spirit. The medium takes pen or pencil in hand and relaxes his arm on a table. He goes into a trance, yielding completely to the spirit force. The following is an actual sample of spirit writing.

August 24, 1933
Chicago, Illinois

The tree in front of us has turned blood-red and it is blood. Every leaf drips with blood. Huge slate-colored clouds gather around the tree. They whirl as they fall, and become darker. It is symbolic of the waste of blood. The deadly clouds portend the battle of the near future when the very tree of life, every branch, every leaf, shall suffer unto death, for as this tree is, so is the world scene and its many branches, its many countries, for every branch shall be affected.

Prepare the way for the Lord and he shall do battle. He shall make war with the elements, and you shall stand. Yes, in the midst of chaos ye shall stand as messengers of peace, love and unity. The battle rages and rages, but by the law of polarity it is met by its own course unto its own destruction.

The Light of the higher forces, God-sent, shall redeem the world. Yea, even as the twinkling of an eye can this be made to pass. Again I repeat, that the servants of the Light are countless—their name is legion. Have no fear, ye of Christ, for ye shall see what ye shall see—miracles. Yet shall ye know them as the working of the Word of Light, for surely one in the power of Light may rule this world unto its God-purpose. So from the realms of light I come—I am that I am. Amen.

By the spirit of Aklaraz through the spirit of Emoah Emoah and Amoah were the two control spirits I had when I was in spiritualism. In the seance either one could be a control spirit, or they might speak occasionally when another control spirit was presiding. Hundreds of spirit messages come through the seances. They refer to God as Light and always contain a smattering of Scripture. Because these messages use sacred terminology and come from a spirit, many people accept them as God's messages.

**3** Spiritualism makes headlines and feature stories in the guise of horoscopes, ominous predictions, and bizarre cults, but its basic activity is the seance where many people can be influenced. And the key that opens the seance is the trance.

The *New Century Dictionary* defines a trance as "a temporary state in which a medium, with suspension of personal consciousness, is controlled by an intelligence from without and used as a means of communication, as from the dead to the living."

It defines a medium as "a person serving, or conceived as serving, as an instrument for the manifestation of another personality, or of some alleged supernatural agency (as a spiritualistic medium)."

In the seance, the "alleged supernatural agency" is the control spirit who takes possession of the medium. This spirit is not the same as the familiar spirit.

In spiritualist teaching, the familiar spirit is a spirit from God who is with us from birth and on into eternity. We may have many familiar spirits during a lifetime as we progress in moral goodness. They are assigned to individuals and come to know them better than they know themselves.

Spiritualists believe in an evolutionary process of spiritual development. Individuals departing from this life are said to migrate to the spirit world and develop there with the help of other spirits. Theoretically, a person could advance in the spirit world to the level of God himself. However, spiritualists believe that God also is evolving to higher and higher planes. Therefore, the best the spirit of the departed can do is reach a plane where God once was.

What you do in this life, the spiritualists say, determines the plane of spiritual development you enter after death. I learned in a seance that a person who lives a good life would immediately go after his death to the third or fourth plane. I was told by my control spirit, who was in the eighth plane, that at death I would go directly to the sixth plane.

That I did not drink alcoholic beverages or smoke tobacco placed me on a higher plane than those who did. The fact that I was seeking to develop myself spiritually also advanced me. Amoah and Emoah, my control spirits, lectured me often on what was wrong in my thoughts, morals, and manners. They even stressed physical health and cleanliness, reminding me that my body was the temple of the spirit (not the Holy Spirit of God).

People who live very sinful lives would be earthbound spirits when they die, we were told. Other spirits would come to their assistance, show them the error of their ways and try to get them to live better lives in the spirit world so they could begin evolving to the second and third planes. This is known as the school for earthbound spirits. Spiritualists believe that the teachers in this school are the spirits of departed educators and scholars in educational, religious, and scientific fields.

The goal of the spiritualist is to evolve as high as possible by becoming less self-centered. As he seeks to develop himself and help his fellow man, he is graduated from one spirit plane to the next. Spiritualists in the United States generally believe in eighteen planes of development. A spiritualist from England said on a *Today* telecast that they have discovered as many as thirty-three planes.

Prophecy plays a large part in a spiritualist seance. At one seance I participated in, where the medium was a member of my family, World War II was prophesied and the nations that would be engulfed in this gigantic conflict were named. I also remember the control spirit saying, "At the end of World War II there will be no end of war upon the face of the earth until the kingdom of peace is come."

Spiritualists believe that Jesus is the master medium of all mediums. God to them is a universal force, not a person. Spiritualists maintain that heaven is nothing more than the series of planes where the spirit evolves. They teach there is no such place as hell—unless that would describe the existence of an earthbound spirit. Yet, significantly—and ominously for all people who choose to live in sin rather than in God's will—spiritualists recognize the existence of the devil, the source of all evil!

Some of the spiritualists' teachings are similar to the beliefs of Buddhism, Zoroastrianism, Theosophy, and other religions. And spiritualism's rosy prospect of becoming gods over individual realms is matched by the similar teaching of the Jehovah's Witnesses and the Mormons (Church of Jesus Christ of Latter Day Saints). It is awesome to realize the penetration and power of these evil spirits wherever Jesus is denied as the complete and only Savior from personal sin. How does one know that they are evil, not from God? There's only one way, the way by which God set me free.

**4** During a trumpet seance I attended, one of the participants was overcome with an urge to giggle. She tried to suppress the impulse but suddenly broke out in uncontrollable merriment. The floating trumpet immediately plummeted to the floor.

There was a gasp in the group as she cried out, "Oh, now I've done it! I have grieved the spirit." Her body tensed. Spontaneously she prayed: "O thou great and infinite spirit of light, have mercy on me. Forgive me for my levity."

The trumpet rose in the air again and whirred across the room to stop in front of the offender. For several minutes the spirit lectured her about her irreverent conduct. I learned then about the dignity and order demanded by the spirit world from its subjects.

Later I attended a seance on the shore of Lake Bemidji, near a place known as Diamond Point. Autumn had produced an early frost, and we had just finished a picnic before gathering in the twilight for an open-air seance.

Everything was peaceful. Night birds were calling, and the frogs and crickets were contributing their music to nature's sounds. The medium placed a metal trumpet on the picnic table and quickly entered his trance. The trumpet rose and wafted out over the water, glistening in the moonlight against the darkening earth and sky. I sat transfixed in the beauty and wonder of the scene. The trumpet arced back to our circle periodically then settled near the hearers who were addressed by the control spirit.

I was almost oblivious to what the spirit was saying until my mother gasped, "But that is not what the Bible says." My mother was not trained in the Bible, but she loved what she knew of God's Word, and she could not accept something the spirit had said. It so shocked her that she let out this sudden exclamation. Ordinarily, she would have received a severe lecture for her lack of respect. But the trumpet sailed on this time, and the control spirit talked on as if nothing had happened.

I have often wished that I had asked my mother what the spirit said to provoke her contradiction. Early in my life she had taught me things about God's existence, creation, and power. Other than that, I knew very little of the Bible. It was this incident that made me begin to wonder just what the Bible did teach, and I determined to buy a Bible.

Since I couldn't find a Bible in any store in our area, I wrote to Montgomery Ward for one. There were many pictured in their catalog, from large Bibles for about $20 to small ones for $1.98. I chose one costing $4.98, thinking that would be a large enough portion with which to begin. I honestly thought that to get all of the Bible I would have to purchase the large pulpit volume. For some time after receiving it, I didn't realize that I had purchased an entire copy of the King James Version.

I began to read in Genesis. The story of creation was familiar to me, but before long I got bogged down in the genealogies of generations. Thinking that the Bible was like any other book, I decided to turn to the end to see how it all turned out.

I got mired down again, this time in the symbolism of the Revelation. A little discouraged, I almost set my Bible to one side. However, I was reluctant to let my investment lie idle, so I decided to explore the middle, shorter books of the New

Testament.

The First Epistle of John was the first book I read in its entirety. When I got to the fourth chapter I read with amazement: "Beloved, believe not every spirit, but try the spirits . . ."

This was just what I wanted. This must mean there were good spirits and bad spirits. I read on:

". . . whether they are of God: because many false prophets are gone out into the world. Hereby know ye the Spirit of God: every spirit that confesseth that Jesus Christ is come in the flesh is of God; and every spirit that confesseth not that Jesus Christ is come in the flesh is not of God; and this is the spirit of antichrist, whereof ye have heard that it should come; and even now is it in the world."

I concluded from this that Jesus had come in the flesh to be a Savior, and that if I didn't believe this, I was wrong. I decided at the next seance I attended, I would "try the spirits" although I didn't know how to go about it.

I was amazed when the control spirit at the very next meeting announced it would be a question-and-answer seance and even specified that the questions were to be of a spiritual nature. This had never happened in any seance I attended.

I directed my first question to the control spirit. In fear and trembling, I asked if he believed that Jesus was the Son of God. I was so excited that it seemed someone else were asking the question.

The control spirit answered smoothly, "Of course, my child, Jesus is the Son of God. Only believe as the Bible says."

I had never heard a spirit affirm this. In other seances I had often heard that Jesus was a great medium or a Judean reformer, and that now he was an advanced spirit in one of the higher planes.

Before long the trumpet was back to me, and I had to ask

a second question. Since we were each allowed only three questions, I was anxious to make mine count. This time I falteringly asked, "O thou great and infinite spirit, do you believe that Jesus is the Savior of the world?"

Almost before my words were uttered, the answer came: "My child, why do you doubt? Why do you not believe? You have been this long with us; why do you continue to doubt?" Then the spirit began to quote Scripture about believing.

I don't remember what the verses were, but they sounded authentic to me; the spirit quoted Scripture readily even if not accurately.

When the trumpet returned for my third and last question, I reviewed what the spirit had said. "O spirit, you believe that Jesus is the Son of God, that he is the Savior of the world—do you believe that Jesus died on the cross and shed his blood for the remission of sin?"

The medium, deep in a trance, was catapulted off his chair. He fell in the middle of the living room floor and lay groaning as if in deep pain. The turbulent sounds suggested spirits in a carnival of confusion.

We all rushed forward to help him. The control spirit had prepared us with instruction about how to revive a person in such an emergency, and we massaged the pulse areas until he revived like a person who had fainted.

I never went to another seance. I had tested the spirits and found they were not of God. What I had thought to be a great power of God, the Utopia of religious experience, had burst like a bubble. I realized that I had been in contact with the counterfeit of what God has to offer—and I wanted his reality. From that time I began to search God's Word to find the truth.

In my early study of the Bible I had no difficulty believing in God, but I soon saw that to believe in God was not enough. Jesus had said, "Believe also in me" (John 14:1). To believe in God as creator was one thing; to believe in Jesus as the Savior was another, especially when he had to be my personal Savior.

As I read the Bible, haphazardly turning here and there, I came upon a marvelous passage, Titus 1:2: "In hope of eternal life, which God, that cannot lie, promised before the world began." What a joy was mine to realize that God, in the very nature of his being, is a person who cannot lie, who is perfect holiness.

Having established the fact that I was dealing with a God who could not lie, I found in Romans 3:23, "For all have sinned, and come short of the glory of God." Connecting this with Romans 6:23, "For the wages of sin is death; but the gift of God is eternal life through Jesus Christ our Lord," I thought about how cheaply I was "working," as far as my life was concerned. My wage, as a sinner, was death! I decided to go on strike against my employer.

I understood that God in his love wanted to give me eternal life and that I was in need of that gift. I also knew that I couldn't buy it, and I couldn't earn it.

I discovered in the Gospel of John how I could receive his gift: "But as many as received him [Christ], to them gave he power to become the sons of God, even to them that believe on his name" (1:12).

How did I go about receiving him? How does one receive anything? Ask and then accept what is offered. There was no thought in my mind that God would turn me down, because I knew that he had gone to the cross to save me. Having already gone to such lengths for me, he would not refuse me now.

There my reasoning ended, and my faith began. It was in faith that I realized if I did my part, God would certainly do his. I knelt at my bed, determined to begin my praying out loud.

The first time I heard my voice calling to God I was frightened, but I kept at it and repeated my words to God several times. Showing my need to God, I said, "Lord, I'm going to stay on my knees until I have the assurance that you have heard me and saved my soul."

I don't know how long I talked with God that particular October night, but it was a long time. Finally, a great peace came into my heart, and I thanked the Lord that he had heard me, received me, and saved me. Since then I thank him many times daily that he has kept me for himself.

John 5:24 reads, "Verily, verily, I say unto you, he that heareth my word, and believeth on him that sent me, hath everlasting life, and shall not come into condemnation; but is passed from death unto life." I thank the Lord for this promise from the God who cannot lie. I had passed from the family of the lost into the family of the saved, from Satan's family into God's family.

Jesus also promised, "All that the Father giveth me shall come to me; and him that cometh to me I will in no wise cast out" (John 6:37). From this Scripture I received assurance that I had been received by Almighty God.

To this was added the thrilling truth of Christ's words in John 10:28, 29: "And I give unto them eternal life; and they shall never perish, neither shall any man pluck them out of my hand. My Father, which gave them me, is greater than all; and no man is able to pluck them out of my Father's hand."

If a Christian could throw away his salvation or choose to disinherit himself from God's family, then he would have to be greater than God, but "my Father is greater than all." I concluded finally and firmly that my soul was secure in the hands of Almighty God.

Anyone who desires to become a child of God through faith in Christ can experience God's saving power the same way I did.

**5** I now saw spiritualism in a very different light. The Bible taught me the truth about spirits and spirit phenomena, and I became deeply alarmed by the spreading invasion of evil spirits into human life.

Many people think that spirit phenomena are accomplished by trickery, sleight of hand, or black magic. I agree that many mysterious happenings associated with prominent psychics and small-town fortune-tellers are hoaxes—perhaps 85 percent of them, but I believe the rest are actual deeds of evil spirits counterfeiting the power of the Holy Spirit.

At one trumpet seance, to prove there was no hocus-pocus involved, the control spirit sent the trumpet sailing between the rungs of the chair on which I was sitting. Since I was in my own home, I knew no props had been arranged and that no strings were attached.

The question, then, is just what are these spirits and how do these spiritualist phenomena occur? I cannot emphasize too strongly they are part of Satan's strategy to deceive Christians and to enslave those who as yet do not know God. Many Christians are drawn into spiritualism because they assume all spiritual phenomena are produced by God—these people simply do not know their Bibles.

I have no adequate explanation of the marvels produced by spirits . . . but I can't explain Christ's miracles, either. I do have a theory, which may or may not be valid. Since everything is energy in one form or another—this is a basic fact of physics—our bodies, too, are composed of energy. I believe that Satan, who is the temporary prince in control of this world (Ephesians 2:2; 6:12-17), is able to convert body energy that is yielded to him into a spiritual force. This spiritual force then manifests itself in the bizarre happenings associated with seances. While I cannot be dogmatic about this theory, I do affirm the reality of spiritualist pheonomena.

Who are the spirits that attend seances? Are they the spirits of deceased people, as they claim? The Bible teaches that the spirits of the departed dead do not become either angels or demon spirits. These spirits are either with the Lord, waiting for the day of resurrection of their bodies (1 Thessalonians 4:14-17), or they are in hell.

There is much evidence in Scripture that the spirits who appear at seances are rebel angels. Jude 6 speaks about "angels which kept not their first estate." Many Bible scholars interpret Ezekiel 28:17, "I will cast thee to the ground," as indicating that the earth is the realm of Satan's powerful operations, with the help of his fallen colleagues, the demons. Satan is called the "god of this world" in 2 Corinthians 4:4. And Christians are under attack by "rulers . . . powers . . . world forces of darkness" (Ephesians 6:12). God tells us that hell was "created for the devil and his angels (demons)" (Matthew 25:41).

I was never told by the spirits who sends them, but as they oppose the truth that Jesus is the Savior from sin, it is obvious that they serve the master of sin, Satan. They are like the people in Jesus' day who rejected him, and Jesus bluntly told them: "Ye are of your father, the devil" (John 8:44). It is important to realize that the spirit world exists as another dimension all around us, not in some far-off place.

When the medium at a seance enters a trance, a control spirit takes over and allegedly introduces the spirit of a dead person. In reality, the unseen visitor is a "familiar spirit" who intimately knows the dead person. Apparently these familiar spirits accompany a person throughout life, becoming so well acquainted that they can convincingly imitate the dead person's mannerisms and knowledge of personal details when called upon at a seance. In this way even close relatives are tricked into believing they are hearing their dead loved one.

I believe this was what happened to the late James A. Pike. He went to several mediums who told him they had contacted his dead son, Jim, Jr., and that father and son could communicate in a seance. Pike supposedly did so on a number of occasions, as he describes in his book, *The Other Side*. Actually, Pike talked to a spirit who was familiar with his son. This spirit impersonated his son so well and favorably that Pike overcame his remorse about his son's suicide, and looked forward to rejoining his son. Bishop Pike was a rather easy convert to spiritualism, since he, like the spiritualists, rejected the Christian doctrine of the Trinity, and if Jesus is not God, he cannot be man's Savior—nor does man need a Savior, in Pike's view.

Pike's third wife, Diane, was a secretary in a Methodist church before she married Pike. Her Christian beliefs were shallow also, as revealed in her book, *Search*. She describes a vision given her while her husband was dying in the Israeli wilderness, and she says she saw him being welcomed in the sky by Christ and a "host of witnesses." She confesses: "The strangest part for me was to see so literally what I had supposed to be symbolic expressions of meaning."

Diane Pike, and hundreds of thousands of other people, have difficulty believing the extraordinary claims of the Bible, yet they unhesitatingly accept the vagaries of personal fancy or the mysterious manifestations of spirits. This reminds us of the prophecy in 1 Timothy 4:1 about "giving heed to seducing spirits, and doctrines of demons. . . ."

A well-known "parapsychologist," Hans Holzer, tells in his

new book, *The Psychic World of Bishop Pike*, that he made contact with Pike through a medium named Ethel Meyers. The television publicity linked to the release of the book excited wide interest in communicating with the dead.

The familiar spirit contacted at a seance will say remarkable things about the dead person to convince loved ones that they really are speaking to the one who has departed to the "other side." The spirits will even say things long forgotten by the listener.

The spirits I encountered at seances were, for the most part, very moralistic. They encouraged us not to smoke or drink or do anything else that would harm our minds and bodies. Ministers were told to preach morality, good manners, and civic pride. I knew ministers who actually had spirit messages taken down by their secretaries and then used them from the pulpit! The spirits often talked about an ethical Jesus, but never about the Savior who died a sacrificial death for sin.

In contrast to the high moral and ethical tone of the seances in our home, I attended some where the spirits were blasphemous and sensual. Spiritualists call them earthbound demons, and they served to reinforce our conviction that the spirits at our seances were truly from God.

Only later did I realize that the blasphemous seances were another subtle trick of Satan to convince us that there were "good" spirits and "bad" spirits, and that we were indeed communicating with God at our seances. For all evil spirits are demons, fallen creatures serving Satan. Even the spirits who told us to improve ourselves morally and spiritually were doing so to gain our allegiance for themselves and keep us from God himself. Even mediums are often unaware that they are dealing with the kingdom of Satan.

Some seances claim to provide what spiritualists call "new revelation." Certain "psychic" persons, having developed their powers, may very well be able to make accurate or partially accurate revelations about coming events. These clairvoyants, mystics, readers, astrologers, or fortune-tellers use various means to foretell the future for individuals. Usually the revelation will be in very general terms, but sometimes it is specific enough to make people shiver after the predicted event has occurred and they remember in awe: "She *predicted* it would happen!" As I said earlier, much astrology and fortune-telling is greedy commercialism, but some of it is satanic spiritualism.

In claiming these powers, mediums and psychics turn people away from God's source of revelation and guidance, the holy Scriptures. The famous Jeane Dixon claims her gift of prophecy and visions is from God, but she also says in *Gift of Prophecy* that the same Almighty Power is guiding all people, whatever their religion. She apparently does not consider the possibility that her supernatural gift could come from Satan rather than from God.

This lack of understanding is not surprising. Her mother, also a devout Roman Catholic, taught Jeane that "no soul should be tied to one church, because, no matter where we worshiped, the same Almighty Power guided each of us." And it was a Jesuit priest who taught Jeane astrology, which she says she does not use because it takes too much time. The crystal ball she uses so extensively was given her by a gypsy of uncertain religion when Jeane was eight.

Rather than contacting spirits while in a trance, Jeane speaks of "vibrations" that transmit knowledge to her about other people and future events. This is a power mentioned by some Satan worshipers and fortune-tellers. The scriptural "gift of prophecy," in contrast with Mrs. Dixon's, emphasized righteous conduct in connection with prediction about future events. Mrs. Dixon does use her gift unselfishly, but she does not use her gift to teach people about God's righteousness.

Jeane Dixon's understanding of the Bible and God's will seems seriously deficient. In *Gift of Prophecy* she says: "Once you have a vision like that . . . you know what it is to truly worship God. . . . But this does not mean that you can dump your problems on the Lord, without effort on your own part. I get very annoyed with men of the cloth who tell their flock to give their problems to the Lord. God gave us our own work to do."

This self-dependence is the very sin that keeps millions of people from acknowledging they need a Savior from their sins—and Someone who is able to handle the deep problems of life for them. No Christian has God's sanction to seek occult knowledge of future events, and any person who does so risks envelopment in Satan's silken net of spirit enslavement. Spirit inquiry and craving for the unknown is a denial of the adequacy and supremacy of God's written revelation to man. The Apostle Paul wrote that we "walk by faith, not by sight" (2 Corinthians 5:7).

**6** Many spiritualists say they accept the Bible as the Word of God. To understand it, however, spiritualists go to the control spirit in the seances, and the spirits reputedly give the proper interpretation. Spiritualists frequently ask, "Why go to the Bible, when you can go directly to the spirit and receive personal instruction from such people as Moses, Abraham, Joshua, Isaiah, David, Peter, James, John, and Paul—even the Master himself?" With that kind of opportunity, few spiritualists prefer to read the Bible—and hence they know little of what it teaches.

For the Christian, 2 Timothy 3:16, 17 is a key teaching regarding the inspiration and purpose of Scripture: "All scripture is given by inspiration of God, and is profitable for doctrine, for reproof, for correction, for instruction in righteousness: that the man of God may be perfect, throughly furnished unto all good works."

Spiritualists do not accept the plain meaning of that verse, and they distort another key verse, 2 Peter 1:21, which speaks of "holy men of God" producing prophecy "by the Holy Ghost." Spiritualists say this means that the prophets were inspired by the spirits.

Dr. Moses Hull, an accepted authority among spiritualists, wrote in *Biblical Spiritualism*, a book he published in 1895:

"The Bible is, I think, one of the best of the sacred books of the ages. It is supposedly the sacred fountain from which two, if not three, of the great religions of the world have flowed. . . . While the Bible is not the infallible or immaculate book that many have supposed it to be, no one can deny that it is a great book. . . . Yet it must be confessed that the age of critical analysis of all its sayings and its environments has hardly dawned. . . . John R. Shannon said to his Denver audience, 'We do not believe in the verbal inspiration of the Bible. The dogma that every word of the Bible is supernaturally dictated is false. It ought to be shelved away. . . . Verbal inspiration is a superstitious theory; it has turned multitudes in disgust from the Bible; it has led thousands into infidelity; it has led to savage theological warfare'. . . . All these facts would show, if brought out, that the Bible, like all other books, is exceedingly human in its origin. While the Bible is, none of it infallible, none of it unerring—when rightly interpreted it is all of it useful; all of it good. Even the parts which the people called infidels have ridiculed the most, become beautiful when examined in the light of modern spiritualism. . . . In the following chapters the sacred light of spiritualism is applied to the Bible and it becomes indeed a 'lamp unto our feet and a light to our path.' "

To show something of how spiritualists interpret Scripture, I have chosen five examples from Hull's book.

*Isaiah 21:4, 5.* "My heart panted, fearfulness affrighted me: the night of my pleasure hath he turned into fear unto me. Prepare the table, watch in the watchtower, eat, drink; arise, ye princes, and anoint the shield."

The spiritualist interprets the phrase "prepare the table" as meaning a table to be used for spirit manifestation at a seance.

*Ezekiel 9:4-6.* "And the Lord said unto him, Go through the midst of the city, through the midst of Jerusalem, and set a mark upon the foreheads of the men that sigh and that cry for all the abominations that be done in the midst thereof.

And to the others he said in mine hearing, Go ye after him through the city, and smite; let not your eye spare, neither have ye pity; slay utterly old and young, both maids, and little children, and women; but come not near any man upon whom is the mark and begin at my sanctuary. Then they began at the ancient men which were before the house."

Dr. Hull comments: "Ezekiel was considered an excellent medium, but like many of the nineteenth century he makes wrong predictions. It is thought that very few, if any, of his predictions ever met their accomplishments."

*Amos 7:7.* "Thus he shewed me: and, behold, the Lord stood upon a wall made by a plumbline, with a plumbline in his hand."

Hull writes: "Mediums see such manifestations in connection with departed human spirits nearly every day."

*Acts 8:26-30.* "And the angel of the Lord spake unto Philip, saying, Arise, and go toward the south . . . and, behold, a man of Ethiopia, an eunuch . . . had come to Jerusalem for to worship, was returning, and sitting in his chariot read Esaias the prophet. Then the Spirit said unto Philip, Go near, and join thyself to this chariot. And Philip ran thither to him. . . ."

Dr. Hull asserts that Philip was carried by a control spirit to speak to the Ethiopian.

*Galatians 1:11, 12.* "But I certify you, brethren, that the gospel which was preached of me is not after man. For I neither received it of man, neither was I taught it, but by the revelation of Jesus Christ."

In his handbook for spiritualists, Hull concludes from this text that the Apostle Paul received the gospel by spirit revelation through the mediumship of Jesus.

It is noteworthy that to both the spiritualist and the Christian, Satan is God's archenemy. I was at a seance one time when Satan supposedly entered. It ended abruptly, and we were told it was because of the presence of an evil spirit. It is tragic that many spiritualists never realize they are being deceived by this very devil who can ingeniously adapt his tactics to lure any type of prey.

Satan is openly honored, of course, by some practitioners of the so-called "black arts" or "black magic." These people are obsessed with hexes and spells, sexual indulgence, weird rituals, and hints of violence. Spiritualists, who consider themselves followers of God and the "good spirits," regard such people as self-centered "spiritists" who follow the "bad spirits." But these "good" and "bad" spirits serve the same master, Satan, and serve him well, because they each give their followers what Satan dispenses: a sense of goodness and of guidance without dependence on Christ; and a sense of power and self-fulfillment in defiance of God's commands.

As Revelation 12:9 says, Satan "deceiveth the whole world." And in Revelation 13:14, ". . . [Satan's representative] deceiveth them that dwell on the earth by means of those miracles which he had power to do." How true this is of all the people beguiled by occult mysteries!

The Bible confirms that spiritualism—or spiritism—is an ancient religion. Early in the history of Israel Moses warned the people of God against seeking information from the spirit world: "Do not turn to mediums or wizards; do not seek them out, to be defiled by them: I am the Lord your God" (Leviticus 19:31).

In preparation for entering the promised land of Canaan, which was overrun with vile worship of evil spirits, Moses instructed the people of God:

"When you come into the land which the Lord your God gives you, you shall not learn to follow the abominable practices of those nations. There shall not be found among you anyone who burns his son or his daughter as an offering, anyone who practices divination, a soothsayer, or an augur, or a sorcerer, or a charmer, or a medium, or a wizard, or a necromancer. For whoever does these things is an abomination to the Lord; and because of these abominable practices the Lord your God is driving them out before you. You shall be blameless before the Lord your God. For these nations, which you are about to dispossess, give heed to soothsayers and to diviners; but as for you, the Lord your God has not allowed you so to do" (Deuteronomy 18:9-14).

God's severe penalties for participation in the demon rites are spelled out in Leviticus 20:6, 27: "If a person turns to mediums and wizards, playing the harlot after them, I will set my face against that person, and will cut him off from among his people. . . . A man or woman who is a medium or a wizard shall be put to death."

The spiritualist practices that God forbade on pain of death were:

Sacrificing of children to demon gods;

Seeking contact with the spirit world through mediums;

Consulting wizards who interpret dreams and signs in the heavens;

Obtaining secret knowledge through any means of divination;

Employing sorcerers to forecast the future or cast spells;

Soliciting charmers whose powers are demonstrated with reptiles;

Dealing with necromancers who claim to contact the dead.

The writer of 1 Samuel 19:9, 10 describes an incident in which King Saul tried to impale David on his javelin. His attack is attributed to an "evil spirit from the Lord." This indicates that God allowed a demon spirit to enter Saul and possess him. The kingdom of evil spirits is within God's control, though not acting on his direction. God allows spirit activity, just as he allows evil men to prosper, within the boundaries of his ultimate plan for man. God's sovereign control over the realm of evil spirits is further illuminated in 1 Kings 22:18-23.

"And the king of Israel said to Jehoshaphat, Did I not tell you that he would not prophesy good concerning me, but evil? And Micaiah said, Therefore hear the word of the Lord; I saw the Lord sitting on his throne, and all the host of heaven standing beside him on his right hand and on his left; and the Lord said, Who will entice Ahab, that he may go up and fall at Ramoth-gilead? And one said one thing, and another said another. Then a spirit came forward and stood before the Lord, saying, I will entice him. And the Lord said to him, By what means? And he said, I will go forth, and will be a lying spirit in the mouth of all his prophets. And he said, You are to entice him, and you shall succeed; go forth and do so. Now therefore, behold, the Lord has put a lying spirit in the mouth of all these your prophets; the Lord has spoken evil concerning you."

From this passage, too, it is clear that God overrules the world of evil spirits and permits them to do their work when it accords with his sovereign will and purpose.

A unique incident involving spirits of the dead is recorded in 1 Samuel 28. King Saul had banished mediums and wizards out of the land as commanded by God (v. 3). When confronted by the Philistine army he was fearful and sought guidance from the Lord. When no guidance came, he told his servants to seek out a medium who could give him counsel (vv. 5-7).

Having found one at Endor, Saul went to her in disguise. She feared a trap because of Saul's decree against mediums, but Saul promised her protection and asked her to bring forth the spirit of dead Samuel (vv. 8-11).

The medium screamed in fear when she saw Samuel himself—apparently she was used to communicating only with evil spirits.

This is the only account in the Old Testament of God's

permitting a departed person's spirit to return to earth. This was not by the power of the medium, however; in fact, she was not prepared for it at all.

Samuel told the piteous king it was no use: God would take the kingdom from Saul and give it to David (vv. 15-17), and the Philistine army would rout Saul's army (v. 19).

1 Chronicles 10:13 provides the epitaph to the tragic story: "So Saul died for his unfaithfulness; he was unfaithful to the Lord in that he did not keep the command of the Lord, and also consulted a medium, seeking guidance." Saul's case is a chilling warning from Scripture against consulting with mediums or trying to communicate with departed souls; the judgment of God is upon it.

*Demon*
  *oppression*

**7** Demonism is expressed in many forms. We have
tended to think of it as far away in time or miles
from our generation in the United States, but there
is increasing evidence that this is not the case. I
would like to share two letters from foreign missionary
friends, then one sent surreptitiously on the West Coast.

Pusan, Korea

I must tell you of our experience last week. The Bible
women, with Kim Okie and myself, were called to the home
of Mr. Pak, the principal of our Korea Theological Seminary.
A relative had come to visit them and on Monday morning
she became possessed of an evil spirit. The minute she saw us
she started to run away. People had to hold her down to calm
her. We sang "Onward Christian Soldiers," then four of us
prayed, claiming her deliverance on the basis of Christ's victory over Satan on Calvary. The Bible women laid hands on
her and commanded the evil spirit to leave, saying he had no
right to stay in the body of one who believed in Jesus. She
had believed over a year ago, but her husband had taken a
concubine and she was brokenhearted. In her deep sorrow,
self-pity, and worry she reopened old areas to the devil

Once she cried out loudly: "I have been here thirteen
years—do you think I am going to leave now?" Later her
voice shrilled: "I hate Jesus; I will not leave." Her facial
expressions were terrible, hard, and angry. She tried many

times to bang her head on the floor, and once she darted to a corner of the room and grabbed my parasol and struck her head with it.

Hours passed and there seemed to be no change in her. Yung Do felt she could not remain much longer, as she had promised to go out visiting. As we were debating about what to do, I quietly moved closer to the woman and began talking to her about Jesus Christ, telling her how he alone could comfort her and satisfy her heart. She listened and I saw tears in her eyes. I told her Jesus loved her—that I loved her, too, and longed to help her. I continued talking along this line and she sat up.

She listened and began to talk. She said she was so ashamed of what had happened. I then gave her many verses from the Word which she eagerly read—Psalms 66:12, Hebrews 2:14, Colossians 2:15, Hebrews 13:5, 6 and many others I do not now recall. I told her why I thought the evil spirit had gotten in, that her worry and self-pity were sins. She thoroughly agreed and admitted her hatred of her husband and his concubine, which I told her was sin too. She talked freely, admitting her faith was weak.

She wants to come to our Bible institute this fall and is planning to do so. She offered a very earnest prayer, asking God to keep her from further attacks of the enemy and thanking him for deliverance. We had prayer for her several times before we left.

Just when the evil spirit left, we do not know, but you can imagine the great joy that filled our hearts to see her set free from that awful, wicked, noisy spirit. The Paks were so happy.

Yung Do and I called the other day to see how she was, and though she wasn't there, Mr. Pak said she was still all right and had gone to the seashore for the afternoon. This was truly the Lord's doing, for neither Yung Do nor I did anything. All I did was to talk of Jesus.

Marjorie Hanson

Luku, Sinkiang, China

Our last news letter told how we treated a Nosu woman whose hand was terribly mangled by a gun explosion. We learned later that the woman's husband was Lo Pemo, a Nosu sorcerer-priest. Jim Broomhall, a China Inland Mission medical missionary friend of ours, has this to say about Nosu pemos:

"These sorcerer-priests are the only ones able to read the racial writings, ancient manuscripts containing tribal history and incantations for use on all religious occasions. The knowledge was passed on with the office from father to son, and the deviltry of ancient times was thus perpetuated. All the benightedness of the race was concentrated in these men, amiable farmers when not performing their specific functions. They were wizards, necromancers, exorcists, but above all priests, representatives of the people in offering sacrifices and making contact with the spirits. Up to a hundred years ago human sacrifices had been made in some places, slaves offered up by the noblest lords, but now animal sacrifices are made. . . . They exhort their listeners about heaven and hell in which they firmly believe, the one a place of joy and the other of torment. . . . They keep the register of all males born and are in intimate touch with all Nosu homes. . . . A pemo is the supreme spiritual authority over a wide area."

It was Lo Pemo himself who rushed to our compound and asked medical aid for his wife—a very unusual thing for a good pemo to do. Perhaps he came in a moment of weakness; but the fact still remains—he came!

After our initial visit to his home came a series of follow-up visits. On one of these occasions we found that the woman was suffering from a high fever. While making preparations to treat her, we noticed the husband cutting three little bamboo sticks about eight inches long and a quarter of an inch in diameter. Oblivious to all that was taking place around him, he silently moved across the room with these three sticks and a rice bowl. After placing a little water in the bottom of the bowl and ordering his wife to dip the fingers of her right hand in it, he waved the bowl over her prostrate body.

His next act was to place the bowl on the floor and try to balance the three sticks in the center of it. While this balancing process was going on, he kept calling out the names of demons. We soon awakened to the fact that Lo Pemo was preparing to call a demon out of his wife. Upon our arrival we had suggested that his wife's fever was probably due to an attack of malaria, but the pemo had insisted that she was demon-possessed.

The naming of demons continued until the name of "Lin," and then the sticks stood on end. Upon learning this was the demon's name, the pemo placed some rice in the bowl and mixed it with the three sticks—a little salt was added to give it flavor. He then waved the bowl in circles over his wife and politely called out, "Please, Mr. Lin Demon, come out—come out—look at this nice, tasty bowl of rice—it's for you if you'll only come out—please, oh, please come out, Mr. Lin Demon."

Then he moved slowly toward the door and outside, sprinkling a little of the rice along the way and begging the demon to follow him. When he reached the end of the compound, he flung the remaining portion of rice as far out as he could and then returned to the house.

This was too much for me—I was determined to find out the shenanigans behind this thing, even if it meant calling down the wrath of the gods and demons combined. I asked the fellow if he would let me try to stand those sticks on end.

He smilingly gave me the go-ahead signal; but I tried and those things just would not stand. Ralph and Ruth Covell also tried and failed. Still not satisfied, we asked the pemo if he'd show us how to do it. The whole process was reverently repeated, even to the standing of the sticks when the name of "Lin" was called out. But the three of us finally despaired of ever making those sticks stand.

Our next question was, "Lo Pemo, where did you learn this art?" He answered by handing us a little brown leather bag filled with six scrolls of Nosu script containing incantations for use on all religious occasions, and other racial writings.

I returned home that night with thoughts of Mr. Lin Demon on my mind and went to bed with the same. The following day saw me poring over passages in the Bible on demonology and dusting off *Strong's Theology* , and turning to that section having to do with the employment of evil angels on page 454. When old Augustus H. [Strong] left some questions as to the connection of evil spirits with the systems of idolatry and witchcraft, I was ready to shout, "Doctor, if you want some real proof, I'll give it to you!"

Later that afternoon I started to write: "Dear Friends, Were it not for the fact that Ralph and Ruth Covell witnessed the very same thing, I'm afraid I'd almost be willing to swear that my eyes were playing tricks on me yesterday; for I saw something which seemed to go beyond all human discernment."

Well, that's the story of Lo Pemo and my efforts to duplicate his magic. I'm firmly convinced that "we wrestle not against flesh and blood, but against principalities, against powers, against the rulers of the darkness of this world, against spiritual wickedness in high places," and would ask you to pray that utterance may be given unto us, that we may open our mouths boldly to make known the mystery of the gospel, in order that Lo Pemo and many others in this area "might turn from darkness to light and from the power of Satan to God."

Lucille and Dan Carr

The following is part of a letter received by a prominent minister in Los Angeles, California, and purportedly reveals the doctrine of "The Legion of Lucifer."

. . . Now we believe, we of the New Movement, that the great Prince Michael, mentioned in the 11th and 12th chapters of Daniel, is the Archangel Michael, who has foresworn allegiance to Jehovah, and is now on our side. We believe that Michael is the alter ego of Satan, or rather Lucifer, who takes on many names.

First, let me explain that we have formed a movement which is necessarily secret for the time being—a militant organization. We call ourselves The Legion of Lucifer.

Contrary to popular misconception and Christian propaganda, Lucifer was not and is not the ugly, cruel entity he is so often portrayed to be; but on the contrary, he is the most beautiful, intelligent, resplendent of all the cherubs of heaven—that is, prior to the revolution against Jehovah, who feared his growing power and dominion.

I agree with you entirely on the victory which is to be soon by the king of the north. You have clearly identified this power. The antichrist will eventually rule the world. That, too, you have envisioned; and the antichrist, the archangel Michael, and Lucifer are all one and the same, in a trinity—separate in action, but unified in purpose.

That Armageddon is close at hand is, I think, easy for anyone to see, and the unleashing of the atomic bomb points to the inevitable conclusion.

The atomic bomb, I am glad to say, is of satanic origin, a

product of the infernal, and is to insure the final victory of Lucifer not only over the earth, over which Satan has dominion (see Luke 4), but over the hosts and cohorts of heaven who must fall before Lucifer's ultimate assault.

You will recall that in the contest between Jesus and Satan, Jesus, the younger Son of God, was given a chance by his elder brother, Lucifer, or Satan, to share his dominion, but he chose to become an opponent rather than to be second in command to his elder brother. At that time Lucifer simply departed from him for a season and has been biding his time, content to see what a mess Jesus and his followers were to make of the world and humanity.

Jesus and Christianity have, I think, demonstrated their weakness and inability to cope with the opinions and the minds of men, and we are now worse off and in more disharmony over the globe than in any previous period in history.

The kingdom of Lucifer is nigh, and we, The Legion of Lucifer, have pledged ourselves to it, and the reign of Jesus or his attempt to reign is collapsing on every side.

Our doctrine is simple. We believe in freedom from restraint, in the enjoyment of all the desirable and pleasurable things of life. We believe in beauty, art, music, and the indulgence of one's natural appetites, limited only by allowing others to enjoy an equal and similar right to live as they please.

The keynote is sexual freedom unrestrained, and pleasure is the password. Sin is a mirage, a superstition that is erased from our vocabulary.

Ordinary members—"novices" we call them—are Legionnaires. The rank of "centurion" is given to those who have rallied 100 members to the cause. The rank of "general" is reserved for outstanding work in the Legion.

We especially need good speakers and propagandists—such

as you might be if you joined our cause. You would qualify for the rank of general. Should you qualify and come over to our side you would be required merely to foreswear your present allegiance to Jehovah and to Christ and to take the oath of allegiance similar to that required of Jesus by Satan, in Luke 4, verses 6 and 7.

I might mention that Saint Peter, who has always shown a preference for the things of this world, is "on the fence," and is ready to come over to our cause when we show our strength in the final conflict. We feel confident that he will deliver into our hands the keys when the time comes, which we know to be very soon.

After all, who wants to be on the losing side? If you realize the opportunity, do not hesitate to make it known to us by some indication, in your next broadcast, that you want to be one of us. Use the key word "Alpha" in your speech, and we will approach you more directly and less secretly.

I wish to mention the statistics you have on adultery and divorce are really far below the true figure and outside the official number. (The devil knows the truth about it.) There are, in this city of Los Angeles, which should be called "The City of Fallen Angels," countless couples living together who are not legally married, only pretending for convenience. There are tens of thousands of women and girls who are not divorced legally, but have simply left their husbands and families and are working for our cause in cocktail lounges and other places of pleasure and entertainment. They are, in fact, our main recruiting agency, and have trapped more members night after night than any other source.

Hoping to hear from you,

Yours in Hades,

The Power of Fire and Earth

P.S. The Legion of Lucifer does not show its hand at present. Our movement is secret and underground. However, in these

United States there is freedom of worship. Our organization is within the law. There is nothing illegal, or illegitimate, about it. Please understand this—we plan to come out in the open and have a broadcasting station of our own, as we cannot be refused the use of the air in this free country. Our main need is confident and persuasive speakers, and that is why, frankly, we should like to have you among us. . . .

*Overcoming*
*demons*

**8** My conversion to Christ from spiritualism occurred in 1929, but I was not free from demon interference for many years after I entered the pastorate. To get Bible training, I enrolled in Northwestern Bible Schools in Minneapolis. I transferred to Bethel Seminary in Saint Paul and studied there for three years. In 1935 I married Alice Schmoldt and took my first pastorate in Bottineau, North Dakota.

The influence of demonism continued strong among my relatives, so Alice and I took our children to Oregon in 1949. I never preached on demonism in my own church except when the subject came up in my regular sermons. But when other churches had me speak on demonism in special meetings, the demons I had once welcomed into my body in seances attacked my mind and vocal cords.

Sometimes my memory would go blank; other times my throat would constrict and I couldn't speak. As soon as I prayed for help through the power of Jesus' blood, the attack ceased and I continued. These assaults continued sporadically for thirteen years before my spiritual defenses were built up to keep demons from penetrating my body. As my spiritual armor became strong, I was able to help others assailed by spirits.

In 1948, when I was the new pastor of a young congregation at Park Baptist Church, St. Louis Park, Minnesota, I introduced my message one Sunday night with a strange feeling that something was wrong. My mind was fuzzy, and I felt like I was being choked. I seemed on the verge of a mental blackout. Sensing Satan's power at work in the service, I asked the congregation to pray.

They were doubtless perplexed at my strange behavior. With a quick prayer to my heavenly Father, I claimed the text: "The blood of Jesus Christ his Son cleanseth us from all sin" (1 John 1:7).

I wound up that night with a "hellfire" message. After the benediction I hurried to the door, hoping to discern who had brought the sinister force into the service. I found no one.

Ten days later I received a telephone call from a woman who claimed that she and a friend had turned on satanic power in the Sunday service. She told me they had left the service frightened by the Bible text and message.

After the service, she said, Satan had come to their homes to induce them to commit suicide. Mrs. S., the woman calling me, overcame an impulse to leap into the Mississippi River, but she succumbed to the next temptation and took an overdose of sleeping pills. She had been near death for several days.

When she recovered, Mrs. S. learned that her friend had been committed to a mental hospital. That news so frightened her that she was prompted to call me. We set up a counseling appointment for the next morning.

I saw immediately that she was demon-indwelt. The only way she could say the name of Jesus was in blasphemy. She told me the demons had caused her to steal casually, sell her body for extra income, and disturb gospel services for entertainment. She and her friend—she told me later—regularly met on the banks of the Mississippi to worship Satan. They would prostrate themselves before their altar and pray to Satan that they might be chosen to bear the antichrist into the world.

Mrs. S. was sincere in wanting to be free from Satan's bondage. There, for the first time in my life, I prayed for the deliverance of such a person. She was unable to pray at all.

Tremblingly, I asked God, in Jesus's name and the power of his blood, to rebuke the demons and deliver this woman, a prisoner of Satan. She began to scream as the demons came out of her and her body shook violently. "They are gone," she said, "but there are more!"

I prayed again and asked the Lord to cast out the rest. Mrs. S. began to curse and grind her teeth. I kept praying for her deliverance. A second time she said, "They are gone but there are more."

I wondered how long this could go on. Demons of madness and blasphemy had left her; what more could there be? Once more I prayed and asked God to finish the work, to cast all the demons from her. At this, her reaction was indescribable; but the last demons left her and she lay limp on the floor.

Mrs. S. then wept and praised God for her deliverance. Each day after that she called me and we had a Bible study by telephone. After two weeks she gave public testimony at a prayer meeting of her deliverance and joy in the Lord. She had many ensuing battles with Satan, but her victories were great and refreshing.

While conducting evangelistic meetings in the Portland area during the spring of 1953, my associate, Kenneth Raymond, and I encountered an amazing phenomenon. Enjoying fellowship in a Christian home after the evening service, we were disturbed when we prayed by the screaming of an 11-month-old daughter.

This happened consistently for two weeks. The child's parents assured us that the child was all right, but they were as concerned as we were. Because of my background, I started to think about the situation in connection with demons. I kept telling myself that surely such a small child could not be an object of demonic spirits. Nevertheless, we decided to do an experiment.

During the usual time of fellowship after the service, I asked my soft-voiced associate to pray. We knew that the child, who was busy playing, would have a hard time hearing the prayer.

To our amazement, at the very first words of Mr. Raymond's prayer, the baby began to scream and crawl frantically for her mother. I was convinced then that this was some kind of demon demonstration. To make sure, we did the same thing the next night, and again the child screamed hysterically.

I decided the Holy Spirit was speaking to me to do something. I could not stand to see the child tormented. So I audibly cried to God to rebuke the demon powers and give the child complete deliverance with Holy Spirit and angelic protection. Instantly she stopped sobbing and seemed quite normal. Mr. Raymond and I spent much time in prayer that night.

After another week, the parents told us that their child appeared completely delivered from these demonic assaults. Today this fine young woman has no memories of that experience, and she has had no recurrence of such.

While I was at Lebanon, Oregon, associated with Dr. John B. Houser of the First Baptist Church, I was asked by another Baptist minister to come to his church and meet with a group of high school students who had gotten into spiritualism just for kicks.

I went for a meeting that night and listened as the young people told me their experiences. At a party a friend had fascinated them with stories of trances and seances. He told them how to use an ouija board and how to enter a state of trance.

They rented a hotel room to seek spirit manifestations.

When they began to get spirit reactions, they became frightened and cried out: "Spirit, go away!"

Later they started to meet again at one of their homes when the parents were away. After a series of such meetings they began to hear the voice of a spirit. Then one of the girls succumbed to spirit power, and the control spirit began to speak through her. Frightened again, they broke it up. They were confident that I could tell them how to perfect this newly discovered science.

Instead of cooperating with them, I told them how at one time I had been part of a spiritualist group, but that I had now found truth in the Lord Jesus Christ. I invited them to call me for an appointment if they were interested in experiencing God's reality rather than a counterfeit.

About 4 o'clock that morning they went to a room where they asked the spirit "if this joker (meaning me) knew what he was talking about." At that point the leader of the group stepped out and said he wanted to learn what the reality was like.

I had the great joy of leading that young man to faith in Christ as his personal Savior. Before the day was over, he had led two of his friends to the Lord. On the following Sunday several of the others attended the church where I was speaking and made commitments to Christ. The leader who was converted subsequently went to Bible school; he also led his parents to Christ.

There was an elderly man in one of my churches who used to sit by the hour in a trance. I called on him one day when he was celebrating his ninetieth birthday. He told me about the many beautiful sights he saw during his levitation or soul travels. I asked him if he were concerned whether or not this was from God. He said it must be because it was in the spiritual realm. I told him I thought we should pray about it, and he agreed.

I asked the Lord to take this away from the old man if it was not from God and to help him to read more of the Bible instead. (He had good eyesight and could read easily.)

On Sunday I noticed he was not in church as had been his custom. I was told he was angry that I had put a stop to his levitation experiences. God had indeed removed them, as we had prayed, but the man was not willing to accept God's plan for him.

A young woman in Oregon once offered to give me a spirit message by spirit writing. I consented with the condition that we "try the spirits whether they are of God" (1 John 4:1). Since Miss H. believed that God was the author of the Bible, she agreed that the spirit could easily write out 1 Corinthians 15:3-5 if he were led by God—or not prohibited by him. The Scripture I chose says:

"For I delivered unto you first of all that which I also received, how that Christ died for our sins according to the Scriptures; and that he was buried, and that he rose again the third day according to the Scriptures; and that he was seen of Cephas, then of the twelve."

The result of the spirit writing through Miss H. was a hodge-podge—part Scripture and part nonense. Miss H. then went into a demonic tantrum. I asked God to rebuke the demons and set her free. The demons said, "We are going, but we will come back." And come back they did, with reinforcements.

I worked with this young woman for several months, but because she was unwilling to give up this traffic with spirits she was later placed in a mental institution. I am convinced that she could be perfectly healed of this oppression and indwelling by demons if only she would consent.

Sometimes lewd demons trick well-meaning people into following their sensual behavior. I know of a pastor's wife who was regularly embraced by one of the male officers in the church because they were "lovers in the spirit." Actually, the spirits had intoxicated them with sensuality, not sanctity. The deceived woman went to the brink of mental collapse, proving that its spirit source was evil, not godly.

These incidents show not only how serious a matter it is to become involved with spiritualism in any form, but also that the atoning blood of Christ always gives us his purity and power.

Though we are not told much in Scripture about the protective ministries of God's angels, we are assured in Psalm 91:11 that they guard the ways of God's people. All who genuinely desire protection from Satan and his demons will receive it.

**9** "And the Lord said unto Satan, Whence comest thou? Then Satan answered the Lord, and said, From going to and fro in the earth, and from walking up and down in it" (Job 1:7).

The word translated "going" means "to go about as a spy." Perhaps Satan travels around to increase his knowledge of the tempers, weaknesses, habits, and personal characteristics of earth's inhabitants, and then to plan his assaults. Satan, through his demon ambassadors, may approach, influence, direct, obsess, possess, or indwell people. Scripture informs us about many of Satan's tactics in capturing individuals.

1. *He attacks viciously.* "Be careful, watch out for attacks from Satan, your great enemy. He prowls around like a hungry, roaring lion, looking for some victim to tear apart" (1 Peter 5:8, *Living Letters*).

2. *He takes advantage of human weaknesses.* ". . . Lest Satan should get an advantage of us: for we are not ignorant of his devices" (2 Corinthians 2:11).

3. *He blinds spiritual vision.* "In whom the god of this world hath blinded the minds of them which believe not, lest the light of the glorious gospel of Christ, who is the image of God, should shine unto them" (2 Corinthians 4:4).

4. *He binds physically.* "And ought not this woman, being a daughter of Abraham, whom Satan hath bound, lo, these eighteen years, be loosed from this bond on the sabbath

day?" (Luke 13:16).

5. *He counterfeits the genuine.* "But there was a certain man, called Simon, which before time in the same city used sorcery, and bewitched the people of Samaria, giving out that himself was some great one: to whom all gave heed, from the least to the greatest, saying, This man is the great power of God. And to him they had regard, because that of long time he had bewitched them with sorceries" (Acts 8:9-11).

6. *He deceives all men.* "And the great dragon was cast out, that old serpent, called the devil, and Satan, which deceiveth the whole world: he was cast out into the earth, and his angels were cast out with him" (Revelation 12:9).

"For Satan himself is transformed into an angel of light. Therefore it is no great thing if his ministers also be transformed as the ministers of righteousness; whose end shall be according to their works" (2 Corinthians 11:14, 15).

Many people believe Satan to be a hideous and repulsive creature, but this is a triumph of his deceitfulness. My experience in the seances taught me that Satan is masterful in counterfeiting the one true and holy God. In his frequent role as an "angel of light," Satan is ingeniously active in promoting ethical and humane projects—whose final culmination is chaos and rottenness.

7. *He hinders the propagation of the gospel.* "For the mystery of iniquity doth already work: only he who now letteth (prevents) will let, until he be taken out of the way. And then shall that Wicked be revealed, whom the Lord shall consume with the spirit of his mouth, and shall destroy with the brightness of his coming: even him, whose coming is after the working of Satan with all power and signs and lying wonders, and with all deceivableness of unrighteousness in them that perish; because they received not the love of the truth, that they might be saved" (2 Thessalonians 2:7-10).

8. *He steals truth from the mind.* "When anyone heareth

the word of the kingdom, and understandeth it not, then cometh the wicked one, and catcheth away that which was sown in his heart" (Matthew 13:19).

9. *He afflicts and destroys.* "And the Lord said unto Satan, Hast thou considered my servant Job, that there is none like him in the earth, a perfect and an upright man, one that feareth God, and escheweth evil? And still he holdeth fast his integrity, although thou movedst me against him, to destroy him without cause. And Satan answered the Lord, and said, Skin for skin, yea, all that a man hath will he give for his life. But put forth thine hand now, and touch his bone and his flesh, and he will curse thee to thy face. And the Lord said unto Satan, Behold, he is in thine hand; but save his life" (Job 2:3-6).

10. *He indwells humans and animals.* "So the devils besought him (Jesus), saying, If thou cast us out, suffer us to go away into the herd of swine. And he said unto them, Go. And when they were come out, they went into the herd of swine: and, behold, the whole herd of swine ran violently down a steep place into the sea, and perished in the waters" (Matthew 8:31, 32).

11. *He lies.* "Peter said, Ananias, why hath Satan filled thine heart to lie to the Holy Ghost, and to keep back part of the price of the land?" (Acts 5:3).

12. *He opposes God's angels.* "And he shewed me Joshua the high priest standing before the angel of the Lord, and Satan standing at his right hand to resist him" (Zechariah 3:1).

13. *He tempts God's people to sin.* "And the Lord said, Simon, Simon, behold, Satan hath desired to have you, that he may sift you as wheat" (Luke 22:31).

14. *He influences worldly governments.* "I Daniel alone saw the vision. . . . I heard the voice of his words . . . I am come for thy words. But the prince of the kingdom of Persia withstood me one and twenty days; but, lo, Michael, one of

the chief princes, came to help me; now I am come to make thee understand what shall befall thy people in the latter days. . . . And at that time shall Michael stand up, the great prince which standeth for the children of thy people . . . and at that time thy people shall be delivered" (Daniel 10:7, 9, 12, 13; 12:1).

15. *He tempted but failed to seduce the "Second Adam," the Man-God, Jesus.* "The devil taketh him (Jesus) up into an exceeding high mountain, and sheweth him all the kingdoms of the world, and the glory of them, and saith unto him, All these things will I give thee, if thou wilt fall down and worship me. Then saith Jesus unto him, Get thee hence, Satan; for it is written, Thou shalt worship the Lord thy God, and him only shalt thou serve. Then the devil leaveth him, and, behold, angels came and ministered unto him" (Matthew 4:8-11).

That Satan is a deceiver of people is indicated throughout Scripture. Initially he deceived Eve, with the result that the human race fell into sin and became the enemy of God and righteousness. Satan, speaking through a beautiful serpent, promised knowledge that would make Eve "like God" if she would eat the fruit of the tree forbidden by God. Eve believed Satan—and satisfied her curiosity—instead of believing God, and she became a sinner, alienated in spirit from God, and destined to disobey God again and again, and to suffer for it, just as all her descendants would inevitably do.

Satan tried to sabotage the development of Israel, God's specially chosen people, but he could not keep them under bondage in Egypt. Israel finally reached the land promised by God, but there they were again deceived and seduced by their spirit-worshiping, degenerate neighbors.

Israel's King Saul was inspired by Satan's evil spirit to try to kill David, the ancestor of the promised Messiah, Jesus.

God thwarted Satan's plan.

Satan tried to destroy the life of Jesus Christ before he could die for the sins of mankind on the cross. But King Herod's slaughter of infant rivals to his throne missed Jesus.

During Christ's life on earth, Satan tried continually to divert him from the plan of God the Father. But Jesus lived without sinning (Hebrews 4:15), died in the appointed way (John 10:17,18), and rose triumphant over death and sin, the first of multitudes to be resurrected to eternal life with God (Colossians 1:18).

Satan's campaign has always been as virulent against God's people as against people without faith.

Since Satan cannot attack God directly, he attacks God through Christians. Whenever God's people fail to serve him faithfully, Satan rejoices in his victories.

Many Christians are "devoured" by worldly interests that distract them from spiritual service to God.

The Christian Church, rather than exercising the power God offers, struggles to maintain at least the appearance of progress. An army doesn't win battles by merely "holding the fort," but the Church of God is ill-equipped to storm the citadels of her enemy.

Many young men who wanted to serve God as a pastor, missionary, youth minister, or Christian education director have turned to other fields because of ungodly church members who brought shame to Christ and his service. Some have been repelled by cannibal-like criticism of Christian workers, and Satan's cause is served.

Satan schemes to devour Christians by sensuality. He is alert to tempt men and women, single and married, pastors and laymen, into sinful sexual relationships that will ruin families and careers and defame the name of Christ. Satan has led unwary souls into illicit sex that seems to be natural, right, and fulfilling—for a time. The disaster is recognized too late by the betrayed Christian. Since the Christian's body is the temple of the Holy Spirit, its desecration causes far-reaching consequences.

Some Christians are deceived by the spirits' praise of the ethical Christ. Spirits in seances say, "Live a good life; follow the steps of the master; learn the principles of Jesus, the great psychic and greatest medium of all."

Satan appreciates an ethical gospel that ignores the necessity of a Savior. Christians who emphasize conduct as their creed will give very little trouble to Satan. They will struggle and fret through life, seldom helping anyone else to find the true way to God.

Christians who fail to grow in their faith are easy targets for Satan. Unprepared for Satan's snares and signals, they have little defense against his suggestions to their mind. Numerous Bible passages—such as Acts 5:1-4; 1 Chronicles 21:1; 2 Corinthians 11:3; 1 Thessalonians 3:5—demonstrate Satan's access to the minds of Christians. Our minds, therefore, are spiritual battlegrounds where we win or lose against Satan.

As the father and master of all persons who have not surrendered their lives to God, Satan influences world events through his spiritual children. In his attempt to frustrate God's plan for mankind, Satan will sway human events until God says: "The testing of man is ended," and he banishes Satan to everlasting punishment.

In Matthew 24 Jesus describes the terrible suffering of mankind near the end of human history. The unparalleled horrors are imposed by Satan and his followers and by the punishing judgments of God. Then Jesus Christ will reappear from heaven to end the time of tribulation and become earth's full potentate, the Lord of lords and King of kings. Then Isaiah's prophecy will be fulfilled:

"And the government shall be upon his shoulder; and his name shall be called wonderful Counsellor, The mighty God,

The everlasting Father, the Prince of Peace. Of the increase of his government there shall be no end, upon the throne of David, and upon his kingdom, to order it, and to establish it with judgment and with justice from henceforth even forever" (Isaiah 9:6, 7).

Satan's final revolt will be permitted after the thousand-year rule of Christ, when the devil once more enlists the support of men and women who still prefer self-rule to surrender to Christ.

"And when the thousand years are expired, Satan shall be loosed out of his prison. And shall go out to deceive the nations which are in the four quarters of the earth. . . . And they . . . compassed the camp of the saints about, and the beloved city; and fire came down from God out of heaven, and devoured them. And the devil that deceived them was cast into the lake of fire and brimstone, where the beast and the false prophet are, and shall be tormented day and night for ever and ever. . . . And death and hell were cast into the lake of fire. This is the second death" (Revelation 20:7-10, 14).

Satan's revolution is ended. And all his followers, respectable and depraved, who with Satan chose to follow their own plans instead of God's, are doomed to share hell with their spiritual father.

Meanwhile, in view of the power and knowledge of this spiritual enemy, what can mere human beings do? "Submit yourselves therefore to God. Resist the devil, and he will flee from you" (James 4:7). Note that it is useless to try to resist the devil unless you have first submitted yourself to God!

*Battle*
*strategy*

# 10

The Apostle Paul clearly warned Christians that they are engaged in spiritual warfare.

"For we wrestle not against flesh and blood, but against principalities, against powers, against the rulers of the darkness of this world, against spiritual wickedness in high places" (Ephesians 6:12).

In view of Satan's power and guile, it is dangerous for a Christian to remain spiritually unguarded. God has provided spiritual armor which will protect the Christian from his enemy. "Wherefore take unto you the whole armor of God, that ye may be able to withstand in the evil day, and having done all, to stand. Stand therefore, having your loins girt about with truth, and having on the breastplate of righteousness; and your feet shod with the preparation of the gospel of peace; above all, taking the shield of faith, wherewith ye shall be able to quench all the fiery darts of the wicked. And take the helmet of salvation, and the Sword of the Spirit, which is the Word of God, praying always with all prayer and supplication in the Spirit, and watching thereunto with all perseverance and supplication for all saints" (6:13-18).

Truth, righteousness, the gospel, faith, salvation, the Word of God, and prayer are listed as our armor and weapon in this battle. These, obviously, are the possessions of mature Christians, not infants in faith.

Almost every Christian has been repeatedly urged to build his spiritual strength, and most make a few halfhearted attempts and then give up—they haven't sensed the spiritual battle around them. There is only one way to cope with the spiritual realities surging beneath the visible surfaces of life: know the revelations in God's Word and live by them. This requires, primarily, diligent Bible study and prayer.

You will need three simple tools: a good reference Bible, a concordance, and a Bible dictionary for study. Daily Bible study is essential: your mind and heart must feed on God's Word and digest it in your subconscious to fortify your spirit. As Jesus said when Satan tempted him, "Man shall not live by bread alone, but by every word that proceedeth out of the mouth of God" (Matthew 4:4). Read a good book on Bible study methods to get started—then keep studying at all costs! You cannot overcome Satan consistently without this.

Every Christian must develop a buoyant prayer life. Special efforts are necessary at first to combat laziness, distractions, and slow progress, but if persevered in, prayer becomes like breathing, a spontaneous turning of your spirit toward God for encouragement, guidance, thanksgiving, and fellowship.

The Christian who is telling others how to know God through Christ will grow rapidly in strength. This spiritual exercise develops stamina, alertness, and sensitivity to our Commander's direction. A soul-winning Christian is a soldier on the move for God.

Paul was speaking of the spiritual-mental battle with Satan when he admonished: "Be not conformed to this world: but be ye transformed by the renewing of your mind" (Romans 12:2).

The mind is the command post of action—the headquarters that is surrounded by the enemy. "The weapons of our warfare are not carnal (fleshly), but mighty through God to the pulling down of strongholds; casting down imaginations, and every high thing that exalteth itself against the knowledge of

God, and bringing into captivity every thought to the obedience of Christ" (2 Corinthians 10:4, 5).

A person's thoughts are like people who populate a community: friendly, contentious, kind, malicious, virtuous, evil, virile, cowardly, optimistic, cynical. We prosper in a pure mental neighborhood and wither in a foul one. And we can choose our mental neighborhood! God, through Paul, directed:

"Whatsoever things are true, whatsoever things are honest, whatsoever things are just, whatsoever things are pure, whatsoever things are lovely, whatsoever things are of good report; if there be any virtue, and if there be any praise, think on these things" (Philippians 4:8).

Our minds are "renewed" by filling them with God's thoughts—the words and concepts of the Bible—so that unworthy and evil thoughts are expelled by the influx of godly thoughts.

When our minds and bodies are tired, we should be especially careful. Under the stress of "battle fatigue," Elijah, one of the most rugged men of the Old Testament, fled from an evil queen and asked God to take his life. It was like saying, "Lord, I've had it; take me out of this mess." Instead, God gave Elijah a rest-cure of a long sleep, after which he said something like: "Lord, I'm glad you didn't answer that prayer; I feel great. Where do we go from here?" (cf. 1 Kings 19).

Tired minds and bodies are signals to be careful. Christians cannot function at high efficiency when they are overtired, just as soldiers cannot. Our weariness usually comes from overattention to worldly concerns. Paul, a conquering Christian warrior, told Timothy:

"No man that warreth entangleth himself with the affairs of this life" (2 Timothy 2:4).

Here are some strengthening activities for your mind: 1)

read the Bible and pray; 2) read good Christian literature that expands your soul; 3) relax with good music; 4) share in Christian fellowship; 5) concentrate periodically on physical labor, recreation, or diversion; 6) spend time in a hobby; 7) remember often to praise God and to thank him for every good gift and testing he sends.

A special spiritual ministry is open to Christians who will pray for their pastors and missionaries. These men and women who are almost constantly engaged in spiritual conflicts often become physically and mentally drained. I have often felt like a rookie linebacker the morning after the first day of football scrimmage. I believe Satan fiercely opposes the ministry of the Word of God by pastors and missionaries, and they sorely need the prayer support of other members of God's family.

Pastors make mistakes, like everyone else, but the heavy criticism directed at them by church members probably multiplies the mistakes. The whole cause of Christ suffers from these attacks from within. If the criticisms of pastors were changed to prayers on their behalf, both the laymen and pastors would be strengthened. A dissension-filled army doesn't win many battles!

There is a ministry directly against demons for Christians who are spiritually strong and properly trained. This is the ministry of detecting and overcoming demonic opposition in another person.

Demonic oppression is not easily discerned. Some people mistakenly blame demons for unrepentant self-will and psychological abnormalities. The source is often not clear, but demon oppression is usually marked by an emotional inability of the individual to do what he wants to do.

When I talk with a person who says he wants to accept Christ, but can't, I say something like this: "You are having difficulty because Satan's messenger is here to hinder. I will pray and ask the Lord Jesus to rebuke him."

The Christian must not rebuke the evil spirit directly. Say something like, "Lord Jesus, you rebuke the evil spirit or spirits, and deliver this soul for whom you died on the cross, that he may have liberty to ask for your mercy and salvation."

I cannot recall a case when, having prayed that way, the person did not respond in repentance, usually with tears accompanying the release from Satan's hold. The majority of seekers who need this deliverance are not aware of their satanic oppressor.

This ministry is not for everyone, but it is for more Christians than are using it. As satanic activity increases in our spiritually starving world, Christians must channel more of Christ's power into besieged lives.

Remember: the child of God is saved (John 1:12), sealed by the Holy Spirit (Ephesians 1:13), seated with Christ (Ephesians 2:6), sanctified or set apart from evil (1 Corinthians 1:2), and sent to the needy (Matthew 9:38). The Christian who lives close to the cross of Christ can have victory after victory over the forces of Satan and glorify God in joyful, fruitful daily living.

**11** During my twenty years of speaking in churches about my experiences in spiritualism, certain questions were asked over and over again. Some require long answers, but here I present brief, practical answers to some of the more important questions which have not been discussed earlier in this book.

*1. Why did God create the devil?*

According to Ezekiel 28:11-18, God did not create the devil as such. Lucifer, one of God's mighty cherubs, rebelled against him and became the devil. Satan is thus the product of his own evil choice.

God created a superbly beautiful and wise being and invested him with power above all the other created beings. His name, Lucifer, means "son of the morning," "bright and shining one," or "light bearer." He had many angels at his beck and call and was prince over all the earth. A free moral agent with the power of choice, he was filled with an ambition to which he had no right—to rise above God. Unwilling to rule over the world as a vice-general under God, he became "Satan," meaning "adversary" or opponent.

The passage in Ezekiel on which our knowledge of Satan's origin is derived is on the surface a prophecy concerning Sidon. But here, as in Isaiah 14:12-17, the language goes beyond the earthly prince of Tyre to Satan (called Lucifer in Isaiah 14), who inspires pomp and pride in earthly rulers.

Read Ezekiel 28 for a picture of his unfallen state; his fall is recorded in Isaiah 14.

*2. From time to time the Bible says "devils" were cast out; is there more than one devil?*

There is only one devil; there are many demons. When the King James Version of the Bible talks about casting out devils, it should say "demons," as some of the modern translations do.

*3. Are there healing meetings in spiritualism?*

Yes. Every seance group I have been familiar with has healing meetings. Usually the medium touches the affected areas, moves his hands down over the area of pain, then quickly removes them in a sweeping motion. This action is completed with a snap of hands and wrists, as though the pain were actually being withdrawn.

I have never witnessed, however, nor am I aware of, any cases of complete healing. I have seen people helped temporarily, but not permanently. Just how far God has permitted Satan to extend himself in the area of healing, I cannot say.

Mesmer, one of the first to discover this source of spirit power more than one hundred years ago, was acclaimed as a great healer. He washed his hands and arms after each "healing," assuming he thereby avoided possible contamination.

*4. Do some people have more "magical" or spiritual powers than others?*

We are all different, and therefore no two people respond in the same way. I was taught by a spirit that my "soul force" would be greatly affected by what I did or did not eat. Mediums with strong powers are strict vegetarians (psychic Jeane Dixon eats almost no meat). Their main diet is celery, carrot juice, and fruit. We were taught in the seance that Adam and Eve were vegetarians.

*5. What is fire-walking, as it is practiced in some parts of the world today?*

For centuries fire-walking has been considered a means of spiritual purification and authority. There are references to it in the Old Testament. The ancients in Canaan sought favor with their gods by walking on fiery-hot stones. It is still practiced in secret religious rites among certain tribes in India and Africa.

The fire-walker enters a trance before he starts across the hot coals. There is nothing fake about this—he literally walks on hot coals of fire or, sometimes, on a lava flow. Having finished the course, he is recognized as having been accepted by a god and having great spiritual power.

6. *Is there any record in the Bible of direct competition between the power of God and the power of Satan?*

Yes. The experience of Moses and Aaron with the magicians of Egypt (Exodus 7:8-12) is an example of this. When Aaron's rod was turned into a serpent, the magicians did likewise with theirs. But Aaron's serpent swallowed theirs, demonstrating God's sovereignty.

7. *Is there a "spiritual" reason why some dogs and cats shy away from some people but warm up to others?*

I was told by a control spirit at a seance that every person gives forth a vibration that can not only be felt by some people with psychic power, but which can be seen by animals. These psychic vibrations supposedly indicate a person's plane of spiritual development. Some spiritualists think they explain why some people are introverts, others extroverts. Extroverts, for example, are supposed to give off warm color shadows that can be seen by animals. Some people, especially those with strong psychic powers, can also see these auras of light.

8. *Do all spiritualists respect the Bible?*

Like all non-Christians, spiritualists respect the Bible as far as it is useful to them. Moses Hull, previously quoted, claimed the Bible as the work of mediums. First Corinthians is considered the greatest spirit revelation of the Apostle Paul, where he said, "I know nothing by myself" (1 Corinthians 4:4). Spiritualists interpret this to mean Paul had a mighty control spirit who revealed things to him.

9. *Is it possible for a person who is demon-possessed to confess Christ?*

In Acts 16 the account is given of a young lady who followed Paul and Silas for many days, testifying that they were servants of the most high God who showed the people the way of salvation. Paul knew that she was doing this by Satan's instigation, and he finally rebuked the demon spirit speaking through the girl. It immediately left her.

Mark's Gospel tells of a man indwelt with an unclean spirit, who cried out, "What have I to do with thee, Jesus, thou Son of the most high God?" (5:7). Jesus rebuked the demons—they were many—and refused to accept their testimony.

In both these cases we see that it was possible for people afflicted with demons to confess who Christ was.

10. *Do you think mental telepathy is a spiritualist phenomenon?*

Mental telepathy is said to be the projection of thought by a mind dominated by suggestion. I believe it occurs when the mind gets in tune with a spirit force, or a control spirit, and is projected by a spirit being.

11. *Is there any relation between hypnotism and spiritualism?*

I have not made a study of hynotism and cannot answer with certainty, but I seriously doubt that it has any connection with the spirit world. I believe hypnosis is strictly mental mechanics, unrelated to spirit force.

12. *Are you familiar with the teachings of Swedenborg?*

He was a spiritualist medium who believed and taught that he could talk with departed spirits in heaven and hell. There is so much good ethics in his teaching that he is widely accepted by both Christians and non-Christians. This is the result of people's not knowing Bible truths.

*13. How do you account for the many "date-setters" who have appeared on the religious scene?*

Over the years many people have made the headlines with their "doomsday" predictions. Many are well-meaning, sincere people who believe that a spirit, or the Lord, has told them when the day of destruction is to come. Aside from misunderstandings of the Scripture, this is the work of counterfeiting spirits who deliberately bring discredit upon the Word and people of God.

*14. What are the names of some spiritualist groups?*

The Assembly of the Light, the Congregation of Cosmic Truth, the Church of Paradise, and the Glass Church are highly accomplished spiritualist groups. Each group has beautiful sanctuaries with lovely gardens, making their premises eye-catching attractions. Their chapels are popular places for weddings. Because their ethic is to live a good life—"Do unto others as ye would that others do unto you," and "Love your neighbor"—and because of their demonstrations of spirit power, their numbers are growing.

*15. What is the spirit world like?*

I asked a spirit this question and got this answer: "It is filled with color. There are all colors whereby the individual is made happy."

In the spirit world the emotions of the soul are affected by color. There are only "happy colors" there, no pale, grey, dark, or depressing colors.

Scientists are discovering the effects that colors have on a person's emotions. Some of this research is used in packaging merchandise. The effect of colors on the spirit is comparable to the effects of music on the emotions.

*16. How can we know that you have not made up some of*

*your stories, since you do not name the persons involved?*

First, my basic tenet is the Bible, the Word of God, which I have consistently referred to. Second, if anyone writes to me in care of the publisher, I will gladly document any point I have made. Third, I do not want to embarrass some people mentioned in this book, who are now delivered from spiritualism.

# 12

Here is a summary of the main facts about spiritualism in relation to the Christian faith of the Bible:

1) The fact that a phenomenon is spiritual does not necessarily mean it is an act of God;

2) The true character of spirits can be exposed by their rejection of Jesus Christ as God the Son who died to atone for mankind's sin.

3) A familiar spirit in the service of Satan knows human beings so well that he can disguise himself as those people;

4) There are different kinds of spirits (Mark 9:29)—some are sensual and lewd, and others appear ethical;

5) Demons are wandering spirits belonging to the legions of Satan, a class of beings distinct from angels—some are on earth seeking embodiment in human beings and animals, others already are imprisoned in the bottomless abyss;

6) God has forbidden humans to try to communicate with the departed dead; such attempts result in communication with deceitful spirits, known as "familiar" spirits;

7) Satan wins followers by psychic and supernatural phenomena that approximate the power of God;

8) Satan is a created being who presently exercises authority over his domain, the earth realm, but he can do only what God allows him to do, and eventually he will be deprived of all power and glory;

9) Satan attacks at the Christian's vulnerable points, often

where the Christian thinks he is strong and secure—only vigilance and spiritual armor will keep the Christian victorious;

10) Guardian angels protect the Christian from demonic assaults that God will not permit—the true Christian is securely on the winner's side!

**postscript**

In view of the mighty impact that satanic forces are making upon contemporary life, and recognizing the decline of spiritual vigor within our churches, I am convinced that we must return to the protracted church meetings of two generations ago for a counterattack on the cancerous indifference poisoning the body of Christ. Holy Spirit-filled evangelists and gospel singers are needed to hold extended meetings and declare the precious gospel that is able to save "from the guttermost to the uttermost" and to storm the spiritual citadels of Satan erected within the Christian fellowship. Christians everywhere must be willing to leave their favorite TV programs and their weekend holidays to get back spiritually where God can use us to prove to this generation that *"greater is he"* that is in us than he that is betraying the world.